A Poetic Addiction

By K.L. Wright

ISBN: 979-8-89324-023-8

Printed in the United States of America.

Amazon Book Publishing Center

420 Terry Ave N, Seattle, Washington, 98109, U.S.A

My Addiction

This day to day struggle, full of euphoric pain, the same conversation every day, with a devil wrapped in chains. Blood gathers around the point, a method turned a chore, all sounds of insanity, the ending wanting more. Then comes a suppression of guilt, even more times in stress, firm confidence in every battle, it shows strength within the test. In a chess game, looking to move, to realize you're falling apart, hello exception, goodbye addiction, never felt emotion from your heart. Learning to live a different you, a cloud will get you running, upon these acts, don't get complacent cause this disease is very cunning. A life full of serenity, a wonderful way to cope. I was the problem all along, but it didn't help that I added dope.

Poet: kylelee1

A Fear

Watching every step I take, the middle as I am stuck, I have to give it all to him, there's nothing such as luck. Feeling all this pressure rise, all these scars are real, turning off and shutting down, as fear revealed will kill. A fear I have so deep inside, as falling a crumbled edge, I succumbed to an undertow or victim to a metal sledge. As fire is cast in walking flame, the end is left as stone, being left alone inside or physically without a home. Subsiding demons begin to rise, but angels are here to help, there's no doing this all alone, I'll fail all by myself. Fear alone is followed by theft, no criminal mind is clear, and even after the cleaning up, life bottled up is fear. K.L.W

Dark Soul

Darkness is now dawning, my faith is closing in, this love here is drowning, and my devil portrays sin.

These light eyes are dying, redness bleeding in, my body's on the couch, the devil's in the den.

The walls are slowly fading, the ceilings fading in; these times are surely changing, and there are no chances of a win. My mind is yearning for a kilter, my body's fulfilling pain, and my skin starts slowly dripping, nothing else to gain.

Such perfection of his body, face beautiful and sincere, he was a perfect angel, he's now built with fear. Now this soul is damaged, and will never be of fame; he has now taken over, and only my thinking is left here to blame.

These eyes so keen on darkness, skin crawls at the thought, of knowing he holds the power, lost feelings of being caught. Now angels appear from heaven, now he's feeling grim, the dark starts clearing up, and he will return once again.

Captured Thoughts

I put this all on paper, torn pictures from the soul, burning desires come with emotion, closing doors that turn you cold. Try to wrap these thoughts around it, but no circles in a square, angel and demon on my shoulder, but they also run in pairs.

Put my faith in my savior, and another lessons learned, touch the flame upon the match, the stick I hold is burned. Open the book and turn the page, all torn from the past, redirect and close the book, reel all thoughts there that cast.

Gripping the barrel of smoking guns, blood is on my hands, comparing problems of this world, as a beach to all its sand. All insanity of this world, soul in a box, was instilled there since I was a child.

Supported footing from the cliff, halted a troubled path, nomore talking backward steps, no subtraction using math. Shade has always blocked the light, add the dark upon the shelf, and captured thoughts will be nomore and trust starts with self.

K.L.W

Toxic

Start this with a memory, end it with a stamp, all the miles between us, the details on the map. Put my all in this letter, phone you will not answer, own the antidote to your flesh, your soul a deadly cancer.

Took the armour of my heart, used it for your protection, and saw the mirror in my eyes, infatuated with your reflection. Throw the wrapper upon the ground, my world you chewed it up, measure love in ounces, between us on empty cup.

You're a label skull and bones, a narcotic forever toxic, no more sewing of the heart, no more stomach nauseous. Now smiles start the day, these eyes they never damp, start this with a memory, I'll end it with a stamp.

©K.L.W

©kylelee1

Photo Album

Smooth the plastic upon the picture, memories added to the book, disdainful smiles from the flash, all emotions that you took. A caption trapped in a moment, another page that you turn, on this sleeve stands my heart, a valuable lesson learned.

Pull the polaroid from it's shell, as a shaking memory appears, extracted love from the heart, clouded judgment full of fear. Plug up the cord from the hoist, pick myself up off the floor, start the rebuilding of these walls and the opening of new doors.

All these snapshots that you were selling, like the dreams you promised me, everything envisioned on the surface, isn't always what It seems. Portraying your exemption from my life, holding a flashdrive of memories, a pictorial through shattered lens, no more living in misery.

As I slide the final portrait under plastic, discard upon the shelf, withdraw myself from all the pictures, you're better alone by yourself. Then the start of a brand new album, in my heart you finish last, smooth the plastic over your picture, leaving your memory in the past.

K.L.W

Life Addict

Life in active addiction, problems much bigger than that, as I try to keep up the pace, speeding on a one way track. A stern posture in pose, money a total affliction, too think I had it figured out, it's all life's addiction.

A double sided blade, no handle to the knife, a struggle in itself, to gain control of our life. When our life is on the edge, rendering a place to stay, in all if you don't have it, you can't give it away.

A day comes a spiritual awakening, a blurry sight turns clear, as he leads you by the hand, withholding thoughts of fear. Now that our addiction has burgeoned, like the growth of a tree, to think substance was the issue, my problem was always me.

K.L.W

©kylelee1

A Pleading Prayer

As I Pray,

Please Lord forgive me, didn't quite give it all I had, leaving you so disappointed, my family all so sad. If I could do it all over, knowing me I'd do the same, to see pictures of my family, me,
I was left out the frame.

I pray to be a better father, between you and I, a son too, as you are the Shepherd in this life, this black sheep was sent to you.

As again starting over, I look to you when times get hard, should've leaned on you all along, these deep cuts would leave no scars. As I pray, then I see, who can you trust in this light, stuck in this hole, supporting no rope, no help there in sight.

You said, no more than you can bear, but this weight here like a boulder, lift my chin to the skies, I'll prove a faithful soldier.

Here I am, Lord, please add ointment to this soul, carrying no darkness with me, as I discover your golden roads. For I see, you've cleansed my heart, the world I'd love to tell, it's all just a choice in life, a pleading prayer from a cell.

©kylelee1

A Pleading Prayer II

Dear Lord,

Here chaos goes again, as insanity starts sitting in, was holding your hand for many months, as one thought handed sin. I pulled a devil off my back, one gift so much was gained, now on my feet and looking up, apologies to ones I've pained.

I talk to you every night, but pleading is very rare, loving the light you show to me and explaining how to share. Handed an angel portraying red, a truly answered prayer, tight gripping my heart and holding me up, a flame you gave me there.

All in all my head is clear, with no rope less hole in sight, as I stand in stance, removing my gloves for the fight. As acquiring my last lay of steel and comfort so paper thin, a minor setback your informing me, just take it on the chin.

With crimson red in my blood, from touching on your hem, believe in me, I'm thanking you, for subtracting all this sin. All the grace you've placed on me, all angels holding bells, with the last of pleading prayers, you'll receive from a cell.

©kylelee1

Concrete Between Us

From the concrete between us, to the stale smell of air, sudden life
filled with famine, all discomfort and no care. All left turns in a circle,
leaves body in total defeat, from the concrete between us,
one track mind set on repeat.

From the phone calls between us, I'll settle for the paper instead,
injury of the dial tone, screaming thoughts in my head. All forms of
letters are absent, persistent demons in the home, from the phone
calls between us, alone in my head is where I roam.

Now I'm collecting all your writings, thoughtful words of respect,
sharing our lives with one another, minus the obscene dialect.
A vulnerable heart fully exposed, to anguish settling down, I'm
collecting all your writings, brighter days to be found.

From the jail cell between us, only a few feet away, cracked concrete
of memories, left to relinquish here one day. A cold dauntless, lonely,
demented all my days, from the jail cell between us,
a broken heart as it strays.

K.L.W

The Ride

It's a way of life, forever two wheels, these bikers ride for charity and the lifestyle that it yields. See them ride in formation, also the patches that they wear, a life devoted to their brothers and will die for the fair.

The freedom the ride brings you, like an eagle in it's flight, soaring over the canyons, without an ending in sight. Take the scream of the eagle, twist of power in his hand, if Jesus had a Harley, there would be no footprints in the sand.

With the long hair of the rider, speed of death grip in his hands, Jesse James was an outlaw, robbed all the banks of the land. A dedication to a brotherhood, just a ride for the cause, a clubhouse full of family, live and die by their laws.

First thing in the morning and ride through the night, would trade in his love life, if it came between him and his bike. The bike's natural feel to an outlaw, like an ocean and it's tide, would die for the meaning, but he lives just to ride.

©kylelee1

Perfect Man

Smallest man in his platoon, then the bombing changed his direction, first time he called on his savior and then wrapped in his protection. Love carried no subject of age, only the situation at hand, she saw forever in his eyes, her vision a perfect man.

Dedicated life to his morals, proved that's all he had, this man she fell in love with, the world's greatest dad. He made the decisions in the family, with him she'd always side, s. She will always be his ocean, he will forever be her tide.

His children, he showed them God, dressed Sunday in his suit, substantial family in size, little man he was the root. Determined man engrossed in God, like Daniel in his fight, a family man through and through, he held his family tight. When the day came his calling, angels showed up with their band, we can all proudly say, stemmed from a perfect man.

©kylelee1

Rose By The Road

With a paintbrush of memories, followed by a bucket of tears, came the earnings of hardships, through all sixty plus years. Nothing but the breeze in the summer, a wood stove when it's cold, climbing tree in the front yard, there's a rose by the road.

Cast Iron in the oven, love as deep as the waters well, she's hanging linen on the clothes line, removing green beans from their shells. As she cooks breakfast and dinner, everyday at certain times, if she's not in the attic, look out by the blackberry vine.

As a man of many tools, locked up tight inside his shed, he worked hours around the clock, to make sure his family was fed. From the diamond of his smile, smell of prince and half and half, with a love as deep as any ocean, you could never forget that laugh.

With a paintbrush of memories, followed by a bucket of tears, the house they built still standing proud, after all these years. The Lord handed two angels to us, a love that could never be sold, house full of loving memories, stood her rose by the road. K.L.W

@kylelee1

Letter Never Received

Touching her skin so wrinkled thin and hair as pure as cotton top, if I could purchase a second of your time, no matter the price I'd shop. Writing a letter you'll never receive, as you watch apply to pad, as I catch a smile shining down, a love so ironclad.

You helped raise this godly man, instilled from day one, being one of many children, but treated like a son. As I write another letter you'll never receive, as you walk the golden streets, hope to follow in your steps, a position by God you seat.

As in the image of watching my mother change, carrying a sheltered love from you, wishing everyone could feel that love, if they only had a clue. Again here with a letter you'll never receive, so glad you rubbed off on me, no comparison to that love, if so, all the sand at sea.

@kylelee1

Come Into The Light

Living a life on the dark side, struggled most of my life, as I was challenged to a sword fight, made present with a knife. Like shoes fitted backwards, life steps treading back, mindlessly walking a circle, running an insane track.

Kept doing what I was doing and kept getting what I was getting, from concrete to the steel, is where I find myself living. Then I got down on my knees and prayed for better ways, you have to go through years of rain, to experience the sunny days.

When I let go of the dark side and looked up at the light, I removed those darkened glasses, so much clearer to my sight. Some say life's a revolving door, until you learn how to lock it. Clean living is a better way, you should try it before you knock it.

Now I'm on a better road, none loose life in the gravel, a new pilot I'm flying with, and a much better way to travel. When you feel it's at the end, God will put you in your place, not everything's a competition, we are not starring in a race.

When you let go of the world, he'll show you what youre worth, a new body you will receive and put that old life in the dirt.

K.L.W

@kylelee1

Whiskey Memory

It's just a whiskey memory seeing you come through the door, order another shot of Lonely, and then recite a little more. Thinking I had to have you to function, holding down this corner both, wadding in a lake of sorrow, drowning in this hundred proof.

Reflection of an empty bottle, no strength left here to crawl, it's hard to walk on your own, dealing with this life's withdrawals. The first steps the hardest, but acceptance sets you free, mapping out an escape, in a whiskey memory.

Life in a half full bottle, leaning on something greater than yourself, talking with a mirror of people, relying on one another for help. So many long years in the bottle, pouring everyone here a shot, as I sit in a circle of that image, ending a different plot.

Full bottle and standing tall, everyday life on the stairs, arriving early to make coffee, staying late to put up chairs. Now with a clear mind and heart, no more life in misery, hoping to see you come through that door, was all a whiskey memory.

@kylelee1

Commit one

Getting yourself fixed, one day at a time, is in itself a struggle, to stay between the lines. A head full of trauma and total resentment, having a hard time in life, dealing with commitment.

The past has torn and beat you, in utmost despair, all the miles you put in, all the wear and tear. The mountain youre climbing, the trail that you sought, with a backpack of sorrow, you should take it off.

With a new happiness she brings you, elated and aware, long commitment in clarity, you're awakened but scared. Been fighting a hard fight, ready to throw in the towel, giving all you got, as much as the Lord allows. Now you two have a job, supplied the equipment, it's time in your life to take a chance with commitment.

@kylelee1

Adams Apple

Just knowing that you're by my side, is completion of my soul, accepting that completion in your life, is the process of becoming whole. An implication of your love, gives gratitude beyond measure, on a hunt fully exposed, your heart, a special treasure.

Missing you as I bear this pain, it kills me every breath, make this feeling go away or grant me instant death. So sly in so many ways, poison behind the dart, eyes all so serpent shape, you fooled me from the start.

I swear by this bandage on my side, you will never be again, started here completing me, instant thought turned to sin. You always put the drive in me, as you accompany a different road, knife inserted in my back, dull blade left me cold.

Valuable lessons learned in life, mostly from my mistakes, a strong love will show you that, you'll see right through the fakes. Again picturing you by my side, Satan wrapped up tight, guides the venom of your soul, I'll never forget that bite.

K.L.W

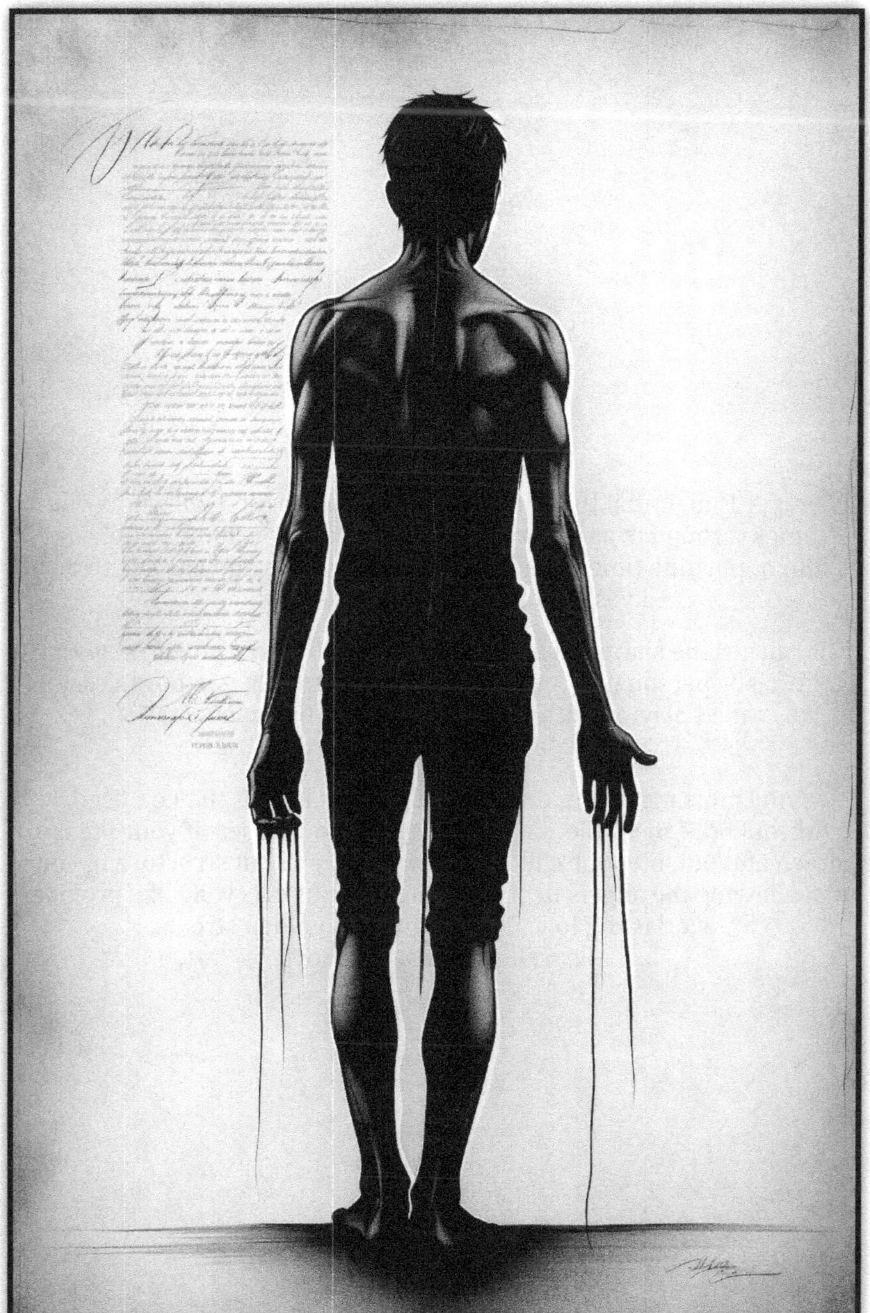

Prayer

Prayer is an initial thing, to base our life upon, God will show you things through it, as in the Bible past has shown. Some people use it in opportune times, others during pain, helps add closure to our lives, as long as it's not used in vain.

It can also be shared in a group or either all alone, powerful in the church or personal in the home. If we don't apply it in our lives, it's called playing with the sword, one on one conversation, speaking with the Lord.

Any morning, night, or noon, communication is the key, used throughout the Bible, as Jesus showed it out at sea. If your life is down and out, lift your chin to the sky, God will put structure in your life, allowing the angels to cry. Adding it to our everyday life, provides everlasting love, he also gives us golden streets, as well as mansions above.

@kylelee1

Sit At My Table

I was down and out, but willing and able, met this man with a beard,
all alone at a table. Let's sit down and talk, as he started to lead, he
spoke so profusely as if from a book that he reads.

He said, I will lead as you follow, erasing all worry you see, prepare a
meal at the table and all sins are set free. First remove that mask, as
you were blind, now you see, just grab my hand and listen;
you are the lock, I am the key.

This very book I present to you, many believe is a fable, you will have
everlasting life, if you come sit at my table. So found of an angel, a
worldly father to you, also has a seat at the table,
is positioned right next to you.

I read of him in articles, as he allowed me to see, the world's
most beautiful angel, was here seated with me. Then we flew to a
mountain, free of any rope or cable, Jesus Christ offered his hand,
said come sit at my table.

©kylelee1

Walk In The Park

Counting cracks in the concrete, as I walk this broken path, trying to put one and one together, it's more than simple math. As I pray to God for guidance, in the distance I seen a spark, this was the first of many signs, as I took my walk in the park.

I was thinking of the spark and what it meant, I was looking for a connection, I stumbled upon a homeless man, on his face a solemn expression. From the tatter of clothes, length of his beard, chambered lonely cries, I thought of my prayer, then the spark,
I seen it in his eyes.

Come over here and have a seat, was the first thing that he said to me, I'll tell you little about my life and the burdens I was fed. I started young as a man of God, turned to one you could not trust, living a life of worldly sins, things of alcohol, drugs, and lust.

Then one day out the blue, the most amazing thing happened to me, a woman with wings appeared to me, I thought it was all a dream. She wanted my hand, I was scared to death, but what did I have to lose, leave this bench and come with me, from that she said to choose.

She knew my problems in life were more than I could handle, told me life of this darkened road, that God's the flame upon my candle. Then before my very eyes, she vanished, all I seen was a spark, that's why the Lord put me here today, to disturb your walk in the park

Standing Below The Cross

Last nail is driven, faced pain with no fear, nonbelievers kept on walking, as others stood in tears. As he hung there all fearless, our sins were the cause, hands high as I pray, standing below the cross.

Tomorrow marks the mark, that he rose from the tomb, cold, distant people, in thought they still assume. The truth lies in purging, resurrection of the Lord, beautiful sounds from the angels, ole so lovely chords.

Jesus showed his talents, others rocks they toss, when he arrives here from heaven, I'll be standing below the cross. The tomb they found was empty, he healed a leprous man, and he proved his existence, showed by footprints in the sand. No matter the time of day, all worldly things are lost, washing the feet of Jesus Christ, standing below the cross.

K.L.W

Throne Room

No platinum or gold, can compare to this gift, a sudden change in life,
some believe it is a myth. Beautiful angels I am surrounded by, chair
so substantial in size, now graced with his presence,
as tears fill my eyes.

Living this life guided by judgment, calm hems create a tune, he sits
there almighty, as I enter the throne room. So much beauty filled the
room, all so precious gems, seeing this road to forever,
the beginning of where it stems.

A gracious float as I walk, under me there is no ground, was lost so
many years, chains no longer bound. As I rise to give him honor, my
life is released of doom, as I watch my heart open,
like a monarch in it's bloom.

Worldly temptations left in the past, as he promises out his hand,
you will never walk alone, remember the footprints in the sand. With
your attention now in my hands, forget the steps in the dunes, roads
now covered in gold, as you enter the throne room.

K.L.W

@kylelee1

Little Things

As I rise in the early morning, thoughts dreadful of the day, when that person comes into your life, don't know how to act or what to say. Speechless and lost for words, a puppet on a string, putting thanks up above, for all the little things.

Strikes you with amazement, home run off the bat, close your eyes and wonder, do I deserve all that. Feelings are unexplainable, butterflies in a box, like freedom of a bird, that flies upon the flocks.

You find that true beauty, inside and out, yourself like the paperboy, dedicated to his route. Then you pray for forever, comes beauty with some wings, this blessing forever grateful, loving the little things. Place grace upon this angel, in heaven one day she'll sing, with growth all so beautiful, thanks to the little things.

©kylelee1

Paper Heart

From an ink pen of thoughts, as the paper formed a heart, was the symptom of your love, it was written on the chart. Drawing out all these feelings, unrolled blueprints of our start, drafting the imprints of your lips, tracing this paper heart.

Secrets are sealed in the tape, emotions inside the box, reads breakable items on the side and fragile across the top. As the box is opened up, holding the blueprints and the chart, underneath the sets of documents, lies a folded paper heart.

Shavings of lead litter the floor, this pencils explaining you, you,re adding color to this paper, painting a love so true. The full unfolding of the canvas, proves the hardest part, admiring every shred of you, loving your paper heart.

From this ink pen of thoughts, you took the paper from the heart, added repairs to what's broken, a true work of art. Publish the story of our love, you were the writer from the start; I found a cure in your love, you put the beat back in my heart.

©kylelee1

About You

If I wrote a song about you, it would have never ending chords, blue eyes that hold me hostage, vocabulary that lost for words. Gain function from your rhythm, words cherished from end to start, your the drummer holding drumsticks, an orchestrated beat to my heart.

If I wrote a novel about you, it would contain a love that's real, an incarcerated stitch of feelings, an absconded heart you steal. This story would require squeals, that would go on forever more, you give me the wind in flying, allowing these wings to soar.

Suppose I wrote a poem about you, description of angels from above, every sentence explaining your beauty, a gorgeous heart full of love. Think of the hard road you've traveled, crossing paths for certain reasons, heartfelt feelings in change, like the sequence of seasons.

As I write a biography about you, the halo about your head, if you are my guardian angel, hang your wings above my bed. Like the roots surrounding a tree, overtime hearts start to tangle, growing strong in this love, as I hold hands with an angel.

©kylelee1

World In My Hands

The entangling of four fingers, forget the ball and glove; nothing better than the feelings you bring, asphyxiated with pure love. Lovely fingers I desire caressing, next to the cardinal holds the band, in this life you get my all, with the world in my hands.

When away parts are missing, trying to accept this half a chest, your appearance needed every minute, as I cope doing my best. I cherish every second with you; you're building a stronger man, to remember you prayed me here...the world in my hands.

These hands are old and damaged, been through hell a couple of times, the enduring pain that they carry,
erase from your beautiful shine.

As your touch takes my breath, I'm your world's biggest fan, as you hold me....I hope you feel, the world in your hands.

He gives us tests and obstacles, expecting of our best, you give me breath and make me laugh, you fulfill this half a chest. Old and gray holding hands, so proud I never ran, everything you have perfected, giving me the world in my hands.

©kylelee1

Britt you are my life...

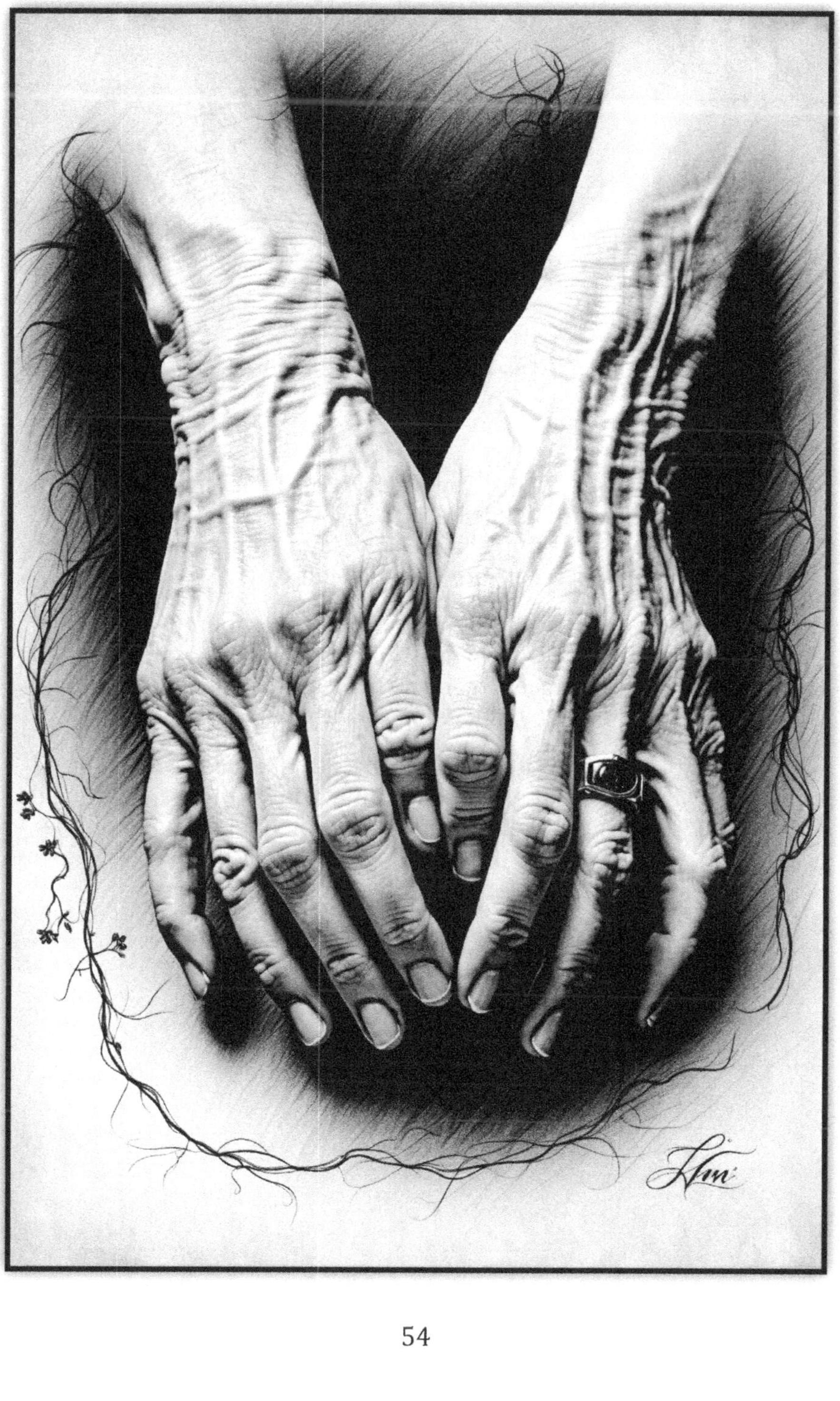

Behind You

As I pray for you every night, God bestows me a blessing, do I deserve this kind of love, with hands I desire caressing. Much beauty deep inside and out, a smile that changes my day, feelings of love so deep and true, nothing much left to say.

Touch of your hand, the smell of your skin, goosebumps from your brand, small things as little can be, a huge ocean to its sand. Watching you grow everyday, grace beyond so true, making me better as days go by, started here with you.

As we wait to see our future, as fate already succeeds, wanna grow old to tell about it, see it grow... our family tree. With so much to talk about, with stories we share with all, as you hold my hand on the bed, as the Lord begins his call.

Kylelee

Your Smile

Upon our first encounter, as you float into the room, like roses upon the floor, I was swept like a broom. As our eyes first made contact, my feet upon the tile, admiring all your beauty, hypnotized by your smile.

A captive beauty she beholds, country to the bone, wrapping a stint around my heart, as it's all set in stone. In a life so overzealous, like fire to the flame, pushing life to the limits, insides I have to tame.

As my mind enters numbness, problems seem overcome, wings lying on the couch, where did this angel come from? The sanity of this kingdom, darkness turning calm, water to my hydration, light to a beautiful dawn. As she flies away with heart, as we pass in the aisle, she does it without even trying, all with that beautiful smile.

©kylelee1

Love Vows

Beautiful white dress, as you walk down the aisle, standing there all
speechless, as my face holds a smile. As I see you crying and nervous,
ready to throw in the towel, as I stare into your eyes,
the pastor asks me for my vows.

Mesmerized by your eyes, as you see into my soul, wet lines down
my face, as my legs start to fold. This woman here, promise to love,
cherish and hold, the perfection of this lady,
where God broke the mold.

This love is unexplainable, but every reason to be told, from the
beginning, the start, this hindered heart was sold. I take her here in
matrimony, as I stand there all bold, only intention in this life,
is to love her as we start to grow.

Before I turn to kiss the bride, my stomach turns and growls, right
then and there I finish reading, this wonderful woman my vows. As
we grow old and watching kids, holding hands on the porch, together
we hold the candle, as our life still holds the torch.

@kylelee1

Suicide By Heart

The first cut was longways, couldn't even do it right, she controlled every round, but I still put up a fight. A sabotage of the serum, deadly poison from the start, cause of death, poisoned fruit.....
suicide by heart.

The second cut was sideways, the beginning to an end, slow dissolve in the cap, a beautiful array of blends. Just the torrent off the spoon, has torn my head apart, cause of death, a form of youth....
suicide by heart.

The last cut is fatal, the voice to all my thoughts, tried to reconcile my life, left aside were my faults. Ravage sins die within, my conscience from the start, cause of death, undetermined....
Suicide by heart.

@kylelee1

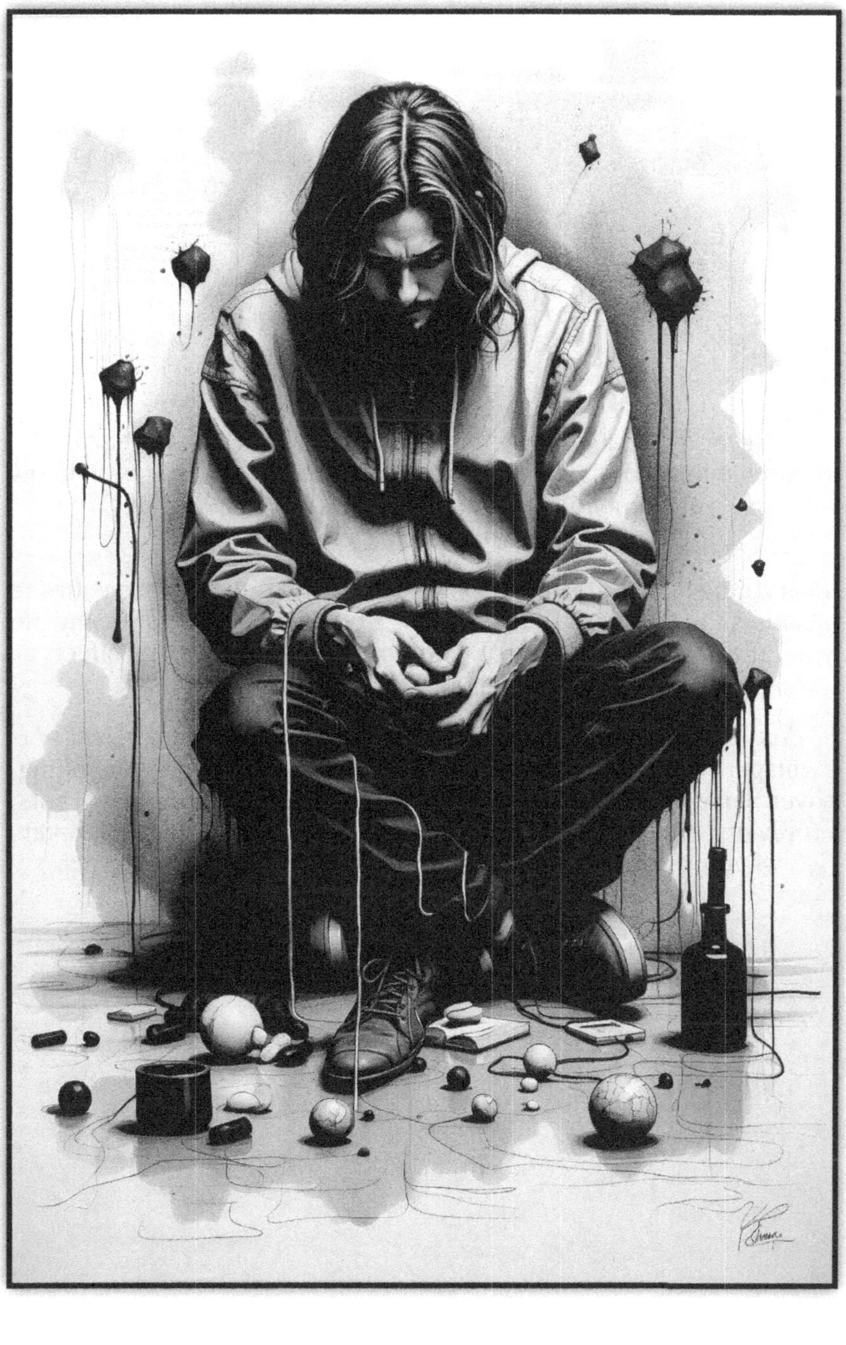

Dirty Secret

Never forget when we met, love at first sight, rocky, sharp, relationship, all our time was spent at night. The more I got to know you, depended on you, think you really loved me, was played like a fool.

Everything lost in life, integrity, love and attire, plain to see your the gasoline, I'm the torch that starts the fire. Every indication in my life, your affection a total spiral, did anything for your love, the effects an anxious rival.

You come around offering love, all in all you can keep it, just a whisper in my life, telling your dirty secret. World see's you taking over, a plague that's cutting deep, potency of the sickle, as it grants forever sleep. Youre labeled a devil's advocate, leaves lives forever weeping, we no longer hear your cries or your dirty secrets.

K.L.W

(Farewell letter to heroin)

Lost Time

As I sit with an empty bottle, my head tears with thoughts, as I reach out to feel the bottom, as I polish off this single malt. Demons surround me in conversation, playing a game and losing the fight, this lost time has got me nowhere, it's killing my soul not living right.

Tired of this life living in agony, on a road with no direction, mixing the road with a lil' pain, this here has to be a connection. Please end this or take it from me, life corrupted at a faster speed, pouring away lost time, being raised from a hollowed seed.

As I watch slow moving hands, new perception in every turn, feeling completed minus the bottle, life's lessons starting to learn. As I approach time with different measures, on roads with straighter lines, no interest in the bottom, due results from losing time.

©kylelee1

Made in the USA
Las Vegas, NV
24 January 2024

84721835R10039